LIBRETTO

C000003525

Iolanthe

or

The Peer and The Peri

© 2010 by Faber Music Ltd
First published by International Music Publications Ltd
International Music Publications Ltd is a Faber Music company
Bloomsbury House 74–77 Great Russell Street London WC1B 3DA
Printed in England by Caligraving Ltd
All rights reserved

ISBN10: 0-571-53442-2
EAN13: 978-0-571-53442-5

To buy Faber Music publications or to find out about the full range of titles available,
please contact your local music retailer or Faber Music sales enquiries:

Faber Music Ltd, Burnt Mill, Elizabeth Way, Harlow, CM20 2HX England
Tel: +44(0)1279 82 89 82   Fax: +44(0)1279 82 89 83
sales@fabermusic.com   fabermusic.com

———————

DRAMATIS PERSONÆ

THE LORD CHANCELLOR

EARL OF MOUNTARARAT

EARL TOLLOLLER

PRIVATE WILLIS (of the Grenadier Guards)

STREPHON (an Arcadian Shepherd)

QUEEN OF THE FAIRIES

IOLANTHE (a Fairy, Strephon's Mother)

CELIA
LEILA } Fairies
FLETA

PHYLLIS (an Arcadian Shepherdess and Ward in Chancery)

Chorus of Dukes, Marquises, Earls, Viscounts, Barons and Fairies

———————

ACT I—AN ARCADIAN LANDSCAPE
ACT II—PALACE YARD, WESTMINSTER
DATE—BETWEEN 1700 AND 1882

MUSICAL NUMBERS

ACT I

ACT II

ACT I

SCENE—*An Arcadian Landscape. A river runs around the back of the Stage. A rustic bridge crosses the river.*

Enter Fairies, led by LEILA, CELIA, and FLETA. They trip around the stage, singing as they dance.

Music No. 1 OPENING CHORUS OF FAIRIES.—SOLI.—
(Celia and Leila)

"Tripping hither, tripping thither"

ALL   Tripping hither, tripping thither,
Nobody knows why or whither;
We must dance and we must sing,
Round about our fairy ring.
Tripping hither, tripping thither,
Nobody knows why or whither;
We must dance and we must sing,
Round about our fairy ring.
Tripping hither, tripping thither,
Nobody knows why or whither;
We must dance and we must sing,
Round about our fairy ring.

CELIA   We are dainty little fairies,
Ever singing, ever dancing
We indulge in our vagaries
In a fashion most entrancing.
If you ask the special function
Of our never-ceasing motion,
We reply without compunction,
That we haven't any notion!

CHORUS   No, we haven't any notion! any notion!
Tripping hither, tripping thither,
Nobody knows why or whither,
We must dance and we must sing,
Round about our fairy ring.

LEILA   If you ask us how we live,
Lovers all essentials give—
We can ride on lovers' sighs,
Warm ourselves in lovers' eyes,
Bathe ourselves in lovers' tears,
Clothe ourselves with lovers' fears,
Arm ourselves with lovers' darts,
Hide ourselves in lovers' hearts.
When you know us, you'll discover
That we almost live on lover!

CHORUS   Yes, we live on lover.
Tripping hither, tripping thither,
Nobody knows why or whither,
We must dance and we must sing,

1

CHORUS (Cont.)	Round about our fairy ring.
	We are dainty little fairies,
	Ever singing, ever dancing,
	We indulge in our vagaries
	In a fashion most entrancing,
	Most entrancing, most entrancing,
	Tripping hither, tripping thither,
	Nobody knows why or whither.

(At the end of chorus, all sigh wearily.)

CELIA	Ah, it's all very well, but since our Queen banished Iolanthe, fairy revels have not been what they were!
LEILA	Iolanthe was the life and soul of Fairyland. Why, she wrote all our songs and arranged all our dances! We sing her songs and we trip her measures, but we don't enjoy ourselves!
FLETA	To think that five-and-twenty years have elapsed since she was banished! What could she have done to have deserved so terrible a punishment?
LEILA	Something awful! She married a mortal!
FLETA	Oh! Is it injudicious to marry a mortal?
LEILA	Injudicious? It strikes at the root of the whole fairy system! By our laws, the fairy who marries a mortal, dies!
CELIA	But Iolanthe didn't die!

Enter FAIRY QUEEN

QUEEN	No, because your Queen, who loved her with a surpassing love, commuted her sentence to penal servitude for life, on condition that she left her husband and never communicated with him again!
LEILA	That sentence of penal servitude she is now working out, on her head, at the bottom of that stream!
QUEEN	Yes, but when I banished her, I gave her all the pleasant places of the earth to dwell in. I'm sure, I never intended that she should go and live at the bottom of a stream! It makes me perfectly wretched to think of the discomfort she must have undergone!
LEILA	Think of the damp! And her chest was always delicate.
QUEEN	And the frogs! Ugh! I never shall enjoy any peace of mind until I know why Iolanthe went to live among the frogs!
FLETA	Then why not summon her and ask her?
QUEEN	Why? Because if I set eyes on her I should forgive her at once!
CELIA	Then why not forgive her? Twenty-five years—it's a long time!
LEILA	Think how we loved her!

QUEEN	Loved her? What was your love to mine? Why, she was invaluable to me! Who taught me to curl myself inside a buttercup? Iolanthe! Who taught me to swing upon a cobweb? Iolanthe! Who taught me to dive into a dewdrop—to nestle in a nutshell—to gambol upon gossamer? Iolanthe!
LEILA	She certainly did surprising things!
FLETA	Oh, give her back to us, great Queen, for your sake if not for ours!

(All kneel in supplication.)

QUEEN	(*Irresolute*). Oh, I should be strong, but I am weak! I should be marble, but I am clay! Her punishment has been heavier than I intended. I did not mean that she should live among the frogs—and—well, well, it shall be as you wish—it shall be as you wish!

Music No. 2 INVOCATION. (Queen, Iolanthe, Celia, Leila, and Chorus of Fairies)

"Iolanthe! From thy dark exile".

QUEEN	Iolanthe! From thy dark exile thou art summoned, Come to our call, come, come, Iolanthe!
CELIA	Iolanthe!
LEILA	Iolanthe!

CELIA, LEILA, & CHORUS OF FAIRIES

Come to our call, Iolanthe!
Iolanthe! Come!

(IOLANTHE rises from the water. She is clad in water-weeds. She approaches the QUEEN with head bent and arms crossed.)

IOLANTHE	With humbled breast, And ev'ry hope laid low, To thy behest, Offended Queen, I bow.
QUEEN	For a dark sin against our fairy laws We sent thee into lifelong banishment; But mercy holds her sway within our hearts, Rise! Rise, thou art pardon'd!
IOLANTHE	Pardon'd!

CELIA, LEILA, & CHORUS

Pardon'd!

(Her weeds fall from her, and she appears clothed as a fairy. The QUEEN places a diamond coronet on her head, and embraces her. The others also embrace her.)

QUEEN, CELIA, LEILA, & CHORUS

Welcome to our hearts again,

QUEEN, CELIA, LEILA, & CHORUS (Contd.)

> Iolanthe! Iolanthe!
> We have shar'd thy bitter pain,
> Iolanthe! Iolanthe!
> Ev'ry heart and ev'ry hand
> In our loving little band
> Welcomes thee to fairyland.
> Iolanthe! Iolanthe!

CELIA & 1st SOP.	QUEEN, LEILA & 2nd SOP.
I—o—	
lan	Welcomes thee to
—	fai—ry—
the! I—o—	land. I—o—
lanthe! Iolanthe!	lanthe! Iolanthe!

QUEEN   And now, tell me, with all the world to choose from, why on earth did you decide to live at the bottom of that stream?

IOLANTHE   To be near my son, Strephon.

QUEEN   Bless my heart, I didn't know you had a son.

IOLANTHE   He was born soon after I left my husband by your royal command—but he does not even know of his father's existence.

FLETA   How old is he?

IOLANTHE   Twenty-four.

LEILA   Twenty-four! No-one, to look at you, would think you had a son of twenty-four! But that's one of the advantages of being immortal. We never grow old! Is he pretty?

IOLANTHE   He's extremely pretty, but he's inclined to be stout.

ALL   (*disappointed*). Oh!

QUEEN   I see no objection to stoutness, in moderation.

CELIA   And what is he?

IOLANTHE   He's an Arcadian shepherd—and he loves Phyllis, a Ward in Chancery.

CELIA   A mere shepherd! and he half a fairy!

IOLANTHE   He's a fairy down to the waist—but his legs are mortal.

ALL   Dear me!

QUEEN   I have no reason to suppose that I am more curious than other people, but I confess I should like to see a person who is a fairy down to the waist, but whose legs are mortal.

IOLANTHE   Nothing easier, for here he comes!

Enter STREPHON, singing and dancing and playing on a flageolet. He does not see the Fairies, who retire up stage as he enters.

Music No. 3 ENTRANCE OF STREPHON. SOLO. (Strephon, & Chorus of Fairies)

STREPHON	"Good morrow, good mother". Good morrow, good mother! Good mother, good morrow! By some means or other, Pray banish your sorrow! With joy beyond telling My bosom is swelling, So join in a measure Expressive of pleasure. For I'm to be married to-day—to-day— Yes, I'm to be married to-day!
CHORUS	(*aside*). Yes, he's to be married to-day—to-day— Yes, he's to be married to-day!
IOLANTHE	Then the Lord Chancellor has at last given his consent to your marriage with his beautiful ward, Phyllis?
STREPHON	Not he, indeed. To all my tearful prayers he answers me, "A shepherd lad is no fit helpmate for a Ward of Chancery." I stood in court, and there I sang him songs of Arcadee, with flageolet accompaniment—in vain. At first he seemed amused, so did the bar; but quickly wearying of my song and pipe, bade me get out. A servile usher then, in crumpled bands and rusty bombazine, led me, still singing, into Chancery Lane! I'll go no more; I'll marry her to-day, and brave the upshot, be it what it may! (Sees Fairies) But who are these?
IOLANTHE	Oh, Strephon! rejoice with me, my Queen has pardoned me!
STREPHON	Pardoned you, mother? This is good news indeed.
IOLANTHE	And these ladies are my beloved sisters.
STREPHON	Your sisters! Then they are—my aunts!
QUEEN	A pleasant piece of news for your bride on her wedding day!
STREPHON	Hush! My bride knows nothing of my fairyhood. I dare not tell her, lest it frighten her. She thinks me mortal, and prefers me so.
LEILA	Your fairyhood doesn't seem to have done you much good.
STREPHON	Much good! My dear aunt—it's the curse of my existence! What's the use of being half a fairy? My body can creep through a keyhole, but what's the good of that when my legs are left kicking behind? I can make myself invisible down to the waist, but that's of no use when my legs remain exposed to view? My brain is a fairy brain, but from the waist downward I'm a gibbering idiot. My upper half is immortal, but my lower half grows older every day, and some day or other must die of old age. What's to become of my upper half when I've buried my lower half I really don't know!
FAIRIES	Poor fellow!

QUEEN	I see your difficulty, but with a fairy brain you should seek an intellectual sphere of action. Let me see. I've a borough or two at my disposal. Would you like to go into Parliament?
IOLANTHE	A fairy Member! That would be delightful!
STREPHON	I'm afraid I should do no good there—you see, down to the waist I'm a Tory of the most determined description, but my legs are a couple of confounded Radicals, and, on a division, they'd be sure to take me into the wrong lobby. You see, they're two to one, which is a strong working majority.
QUEEN	Don't let that distress you; you shall be returned as a Liberal-Conservative, and your legs shall be our peculiar care.
STREPHON	(*bowing*) I see your Majesty does not do things by halves.
QUEEN	No, we are fairies down to the feet.

Music No. 4 Exit of Fairies. SOLO. (Queen & Chorus of Fairies)

"Fare thee well, attractive stranger."

QUEEN	Fare thee well, attractive stranger,
CHORUS	Fare thee well, attractive stranger!
QUEEN	Should'st thou be in doubt or danger, Peril or perplexitee, Call us, and we'll come to thee.
CHORUS	Aye, call us, and we'll come to thee. Tripping hither, tripping thither, Nobody knows why or whither, We must now be taking wing To another fairy ring. Tripping hither, tripping thither, We must now be taking wing To another fairy ring.

(FAIRIES and QUEEN trip off. IOLANTHE, who takes an affectionate farewell of her son, going off last.)

Enter PHYLLIS, singing and dancing, and accompanying herself on a flageolet.)

Music No. 4a ENTRANCE OF PHYLLIS. SOLI. (Phyllis & Strephon)

"Good morrow, good lover."

| PHYLLIS | Good morrow, good lover! Good lover, good morrow! I prithee discover, Steal, purchase, or borrow, Some means of concealing The care you are feeling, And join in a measure Expressive of pleasure, For we're to be married to-day—to-day! Yes, we're to be married to-day! |

6

BOTH	Yes, we're to be married to-day, to-day, Yes, we're to be married to-day!
STREPHON	(*embracing her*). My Phyllis! And to-day we are to be made happy for ever.
PHYLLIS	Well, we're to be married.
STREPHON	It's the same thing.
PHYLLIS	I suppose it is. But, oh, Strephon, I tremble at the step I'm taking! I believe it's penal servitude for life to marry a Ward of Court without the Lord Chancellor's consent! I shall be of age in two years. Don't you think you could wait two years?
STREPHON	Two years. Have you ever looked in the glass?
PHYLLIS	No, never.
STREPHON	Here, look at that (*showing her a pocket mirror*), and tell me if you think it rational to expect me to wait two years?
PHYLLIS	(*looking at herself*). No. You're quite right—it's asking too much. One must be reasonable.
STREPHON	Besides, who knows what will happen in two years? Why, you might fall in love with the Lord Chancellor himself by that time.
PHYLLIS	Yes. He's a clean old gentleman.
STREPHON'	As it is, half the House of Lords are sighing at your feet.
PHYLLIS	The House of Lords are certainly extremely attentive.
STREPHON	Attentive? I should think they were! Why did five-and-twenty Liberal Peers come down to shoot over your grass-plot last autumn? It couldn't have been the sparrows. Why did five-and-twenty Conservative Peers come down to fish your pond? Don't tell me it was the gold-fish! No, no—delays are dangerous, and if we are to marry, the sooner the better.

Music No. 5 DUET. (Phyllis & Strephon)

"None shall part us."

PHYLLIS	None shall part us from each other, One in life and death are we: All in all to one another, I to thee and thou to me! All in all to one another— I to thee and thou to me!

PHYLLIS
Thou the tree, and
I the flower;
Thou the idol,
I the throng

STREPHON
I the tree,
Thou the flower;
I the idol,
Thou the throng;

7

PHYLLIS (Contd.)
Thou the day and
I the hour
Thou the singer; I the song!

STREPHON (Contd.)
I the day and
thou the hour
I the singer; thou the song!

STREPHON   All in all since that fond meeting
When, in joy, I woke to find
Mine the heart, within thee beating,
Mine the love that heart enshrined!
Mine the heart, within thee beating,
Mine the love that heart enshrined!

PHYLLIS
Thou the stream, and
I the willow
Thou the sculptor;
I the clay
Thou the ocean;
I the billow
Thou the sunrise; I the day!
Thou the stream and
I the willow
Thou the sculptor;
I the clay
Thou the ocean; I the billow
Thou the sunrise; I the day!

STREPHON
I the stream,
Thou the willow;
I the sculptor,
Thou the clay;
I the ocean;
Thou the billow
I the sunrise; thou the day!
I the
Stream and
Thou the
Willow
I the ocean; Thou the billow
I the sunrise; Thou the day!

(Exeunt STREPHON and PHYLLIS together.)

Music No. 6 ENTRANCE & MARCH OF PEERS. (Tenors & Basses.)

"Loudly let the trumpet bray."

TENORS
Loudly let the trumpet bray,
Tan-tan-ta-ra, tan-tan-ta-ra!
Proudly bang the sounding brasses,

As upon its lordly way
This unique procession passes.
Tan-tan-ta-ra,
tan-tan-ta-ra,
tan-tan-ta-ra, tan-ta-
ra, tan-ta-ra, tan-ta-
ra, tan-ta-ra, tan-ta-
ra, tan-ta-ra, tan-ta-
ra, tan-ta-ra, tan-ta-
ra! Tzing, boom!
Bow, bow, ye lower middle classes!
Bow, bow, ye tradesmen, bow, ye masses,
Blow the trumpets, bang the brasses,
Tan-tan-ta-ra! Tzing, boom!

BASSES
Loudly let the trumpet bray,

Proudly bang the sounding brasses,
Tzing, boom!
As upon its lordly way
This unique procession passes.
Tzing,
boom, tzing,
boom, tzing, boom, tzing,
boom, tzing, boom, tzing,
boom, tzing, boom, tzing,
boom, tzing, boom, tzing,
boom! Tan-ta-ra, tan-ta-
ra! Tzing, boom!

Bow, bow, ye lower middle classes,
Bow, bow, ye tradesmen, bow, ye masses,
Blow the trumpets, bang the brasses.

8

TENORS (Contd.)

Tan-tan-ta-ra, tan-ta-
ra, tan-ta-ra, tan-ta-
ra, tan-ta-ra! Tzing,
boom, tzing, boom!
We are Peers of highest station,
Paragons of legislation,
Pillars of the British nation.

We are
Peers of
highest
station,
Para-
gons of
legis-
lation,
Pillars
of the
British
nation.

BASSES (Contd.)

Tzing,
boom, tzing, boom!
Tzing,
boom, tzing, boom!

Tan-tan-ta-ra, tan-ta-ra,
Tzing, boom, tzing, boom, tan-ta-ra,
Tzing, boom!
We are Peers of
highest station,
Paragons of
legislation,
Pillars of the
British nation,
Pillars of the
British nation,
We are Peers of
highest station,
Paragons of
legislation.

ALL

Tan-tan-ta-ra, tan-ta-ra, Tzing, boom, tzing, boom!
Tan-ta-ra, tan-ta-ra, Tzing, boom!
Bow, bow, ye lower middle classes!
Bow, bow, ye tradesmen, bow, ye masses,
Blow the trumpets, bang the brasses,
Tan-tan-ta-ra, Tzing, boom!
Bow, bow, ye lower middle classes,
Bow, bow, ye tradesmen, bow, ye masses,
Blow the trumpets, bang the brasses,

TENORS

Tan-tan-ta-ra!
Tan-tan-ta-ra!
Tan-tan-ta-ra!

BASSES

Tzing, boom, tzing, boom!
Tzing, boom, tzing, boom!
Tzing, boom, tzing, boom!

ALL

Blow, blow the trumpets, bang the brasses!
Blow, blow the trumpets, bang the brasses!
Blow, blow the trumpets,
Blow, blow the trumpets!

TENORS

Tan-ta-ra, ta ta ta ta ta ta,
Tan-ta-ra, ta ta ta ta ta ta,
Tan-ta-ra, ta ta ta ta ta ta,
Tan-ta-ra, ta ta ta ta ta ta,
Tan-ta-ra, ta ta, tan-ta-ra, ta ta,
Tan-ta-ra, ta ta, tan-ta-ra, ta ta,
Tan-ta-ra, ta ta ta ta ta ta
ta.

BASSES

Bang, bang the
brasses, boom!
Bang, bang the
brasses, boom!
Tzing, boom!
Tzing, boom!
Tzing, boom, Tzing,
boom!

ALL

Bow, ye lower middle classes,
Bow, ye tradesmen, bow, ye masses,

ALL (Contd.)	Bow, ye lower middle classes, Bow, ye tradesmen, bow, ye masses. Tan-tan-ta-ra, tan-tan-ta-ra, tan-tan-ta-ra, tan-ta-ra, tan-ta-ra, tan-ta-ra, tan-ta-ra, ra, ra, ra, ra! Tan-ta-ra! Tan-ta-ra!

(Enter the LORD CHANCELLOR, followed by his train-bearer.)

Music No. 6A ENTRANCE OF LORD CHANCELLOR.

Music No. 7 SONG (Lord Chancellor, and Chorus of Peers)

"The Law is the true embodiment."

LORD CH.	The Law is the true embodiment Of ev'rything that's excellent, It has no kind of fault or flaw, And I, my lords, embody the Law. The constitutional guardian I Of pretty young Wards in Chancery, All very agreeable girls—and none Are over the age of twenty-one, A pleasant occupation for A rather susceptible Chancellor!
ALL	A pleasant occupation for A rather susceptible Chancellor!
LORD CH.	But though the compliment implied Inflates me with legitimate pride, It nevertheless can't be denied That it has its inconvenient side. For I'm not so old, and not so plain, And I'm quite prepared to marry again, But there'd be the deuce to pay in the Lords If I fell in love with one of my Wards! Which rather tries my temper, for I'm *such* a susceptible Chancellor!
ALL	Which rather tries his temper, for He's *such* a sus-ceptible Chancellor!
LORD CH.	And ev'ry one who'd marry a Ward Must come to me for my accord, And in my court I sit all day, Giving agreeable girls away, With one for him—and one for he— And one for you—and one for ye— And one for thou—and one for thee— But never, oh never a one for me! Which is exasperating, for A highly susceptible Chancellor!

ALL	Which is exasperating, for
	A highly susceptible Chancellor!

Enter LORD TOLLOLLER

LORD TOLL.   And now, my Lords, to the business of the day.

LORD CH.   By all means. Phyllis, who is a Ward of Court, has so powerfully affected your Lordships that you have appealed to me in a body to give her to whichever one of you she may think proper to select, and a noble Lord has just gone to her cottage to request her immediate attendance. It would be idle to deny that I, myself, have the misfortune to be singularly attracted by this young person. My regard for her is rapidly undermining my constitution. Three months ago I was a stout man. I need say no more. If I could reconcile it with my duty, I should unhesitatingly award her to myself, for I can conscientiously say that I know no man who is so well fitted to render her exceptionally happy. (Peers: Hear, hear!) But such an award would be open to misconstruction, and therefore, at whatever personal inconvenience, I waive my claim.

LORD TOLL.   My Lord, I desire, on the part of this House, to express its sincere sympathy with your Lordship's most painful position.

LORD CH.   I thank your Lordships. The feelings of a Lord Chancellor who is in love with a Ward of Court are not to be envied. What is his position? Can he give his own consent to his own marriage with his own Ward? Can he marry his own Ward without his own consent? And if he marries his own Ward without his own consent, can he commit himself for contempt of his own Court? And if he commit himself for contempt of his own Court, can he appear by counsel before himself, to move for arrest of his own judgment? Ah, my Lords, it is indeed painful to have to sit upon a woolsack which is stuffed with such thorns as these!

Enter LORD MOUNTARARAT.

LORD MOUNT.   My Lords, I have much pleasure in announcing that I have succeeded in inducing the young person to present herself at the Bar of this House.

Enter PHYLLIS

Music No. 8   TRIO AND CHORUS OF PEERS. (Phyllis, Lord Tol. and Lord Mountararat)

"My well-loved Lord."

Recit.—PHYLLIS   My well-loved Lord and Guardian dear,
You summoned me, and I am here!

Chorus of PEERS   Oh, rapture, how beautiful!
How gentle—how dutiful!

SOLO—LORD TOLLOLLER.

Of all the young ladies I know
This pretty young lady's the fairest;
Her lips have the rosiest show,
Her eyes are the richest and rarest.

LORD TOLL.
(Contd.)

Her origin's lowly, it's true,
But of birth and position I've plenty;
I've grammar and spelling for two,
And blood and behaviour for twenty!

LORD TOLL & CHORUS Ah.

LORD TOLL.

Her origin's lowly, it's true,
I've grammar and spelling for two;

LORD TOLL.

Of birth and position I've plenty,
With blood and behaviour for twenty!
Of birth and position I've
plenty, With blood and be—
haviour for twenty!

CHORUS

Of birth and position he's plenty,
With blood and behaviour for twenty!
With blood and be—
ha—viour
for twenty!

SOLO—LORD MOUNTARARAT.

Though the views of the House have diverged
On ev'ry conceivable motion,
All questions of Party are merged
In a frenzy of love and devotion;
If you ask us distinctly to say
What Party we claim to belong to,
We reply, without doubt or delay,
The Party we're singing this song to!
If you ask us distinctly to say,
We reply, without doubt or delay,
The Party we claim to belong to
Is the Party we're singing this song to!
The party we claim to belong to's
The Party we're singing this song to!

SOLO—PHYLLIS

I'm very much pain'd to refuse,
But I'll stick to my pipes and my tabors;
I can spell all the words that I use,
And my grammar's as good as my neighbours!
As for birth—I was born like the rest,
My behaviour is rustic but hearty,
And I know where to turn for the best,
When I want a particular Party!

PHYLLIS & CHORUS Ah!

PHYLLIS

Though my station is none of the best,
I suppose I was born like the rest,

LORD TOLL. & LORD MOUNT.

Though her station is none of the best,
I suppose she was born like the rest.

PHYLLIS

I know where to look for my hearty,
When I want a particular party, I
know where to look for my
hearty, Whenever I
want a par—ty,

LD. TOLL., LD. MOUNT&CHORUS

She knows where to look for her hearty,
When she wants a particular party, She
knows where to
look
for a par—ty

PHYL., LD. TOLL. & LD. MOUNT.	**CHORUS**

<table>
<tr><td>

PHYL., LD. TOLL. & LD. MOUNT.

For $\begin{smallmatrix} my \\ her \end{smallmatrix}$ party

</td><td>

CHORUS
Ah,   ah,
   Ah,   ah,
ah,   ah,   ah,   ah,
   ah,   ah,   ah,

</td></tr>
<tr><td>

PHYLLIS
I know where to look for my party,
my party.

</td><td>

LD. TOLL., LD. MOUNT. & CHORUS
She knows where to look for her party,
her party.

</td></tr>
</table>

Music No. 9 RECIT.—(Phyllis)

"Nay, tempt me not."

PHYLLIS   Nay, tempt me not. To wealth I'll not be bound:
                In lowly cot Alone is virtue found!

CHORUS   No, no; indeed high rank will never hurt you,
                The Peerage is not destitute of virtue.

Music No. 10 CHORUS OF PEERS, & SONG—(Lord Tolloller)

"Spurn not the nobly born."

LORD TOLL.   Spurn not the nobly born With love affected!
                Nor treat with virtuous scorn The well-connected!
                High rank involves no shame, We boast an equal claim
                With him of humble name To be respected!
                Blue blood! Blue blood! When virtuous love is sought,
                Thy pow'r is naught, Though dating from the Flood,
                Blue blood, ah, blue blood!

CHORUS   When virtuous love is sought, Thy pow'r is naught,
                Though dating from the Flood,

TENORS	**BASSES**
Blue blood, ah, blue blood!	Blue blood, blue blood!

LORD TOLL.   Spare us the bitter pain Of stern denials,
                Nor with lowborn disdain Augment our trials.
                Hearts just as pure and fair May beat in Belgrave Square
                As in the lowly air Of Seven Dials!
                Blue blood! Blue blood!
                Of what avail art thou To serve us now?
                Though dating from the Flood,
                Blue blood, ah, blue blood!

CHORUS   Of what avail art thou To serve us now?
                Though dating from the Flood,

TENORS	**BASSES**
Blue blood,	Blue blood,

LORD TOLL. & CHORUS   Ah, blue blood!

13

Music No. 11 Phyllis, Lord Tolloller, Lord Mountararat, Strephon, Lord Chancellor,
& CHORUS OF PEERS.

"My Lords; it may not be"

RECIT.—PHYLLIS

My Lords, it may not be. With grief my heart is riven!
You waste your time on me, For ah! my heart is given!

ALL   Given!

PHYLLIS   Yes, given!

ALL   Oh, horror!!!

RECIT.—LORD CHANCELLOR

And who has dar'd to brave our high displeasure,
And thus defy our definite command?

Enter STREPHON

STREPHON   'Tis I—young Strephon! mine this priceless treasure!
Against the world I claim my darling's hand!
        (PHYLLIS rushes to his arms.)
A shepherd I—

ALL   A shepherd he!

STREPHON   Of Arca*dy*—

ALL   Of Arcadee!

STREPHON   Betroth'd are we!

ALL   Betroth'd are they—

STREPHON   And mean to be—

ALL   Espous'd to-day!

STREPHON	THE OTHERS
A shepherd I, Of Arca*dy*,	A shepherd he, Of Arca*dee*,
A shepherd I, Of Arca*dy*;	A shepherd he, Of Arca*dee*;
Betroth'd are we, Betroth'd are we,	Betroth'd are they, Betroth'd are they,
And mean to be espous'd today!	And mean to be espous'd today!

DUET

LORD TOLL.
& LORD MOUNT. (*aside to each other*)

'Neath this blow, worse than stab of dagger,
Though we momentarily stagger,
In each heart Proud are we innately,
Let's depart Dignified and stately!

TENORS
Let's depart Dignified and stately,
Dignified and stately,

Dignified and stately,

Dignified and stately!

BASSES
Let's depart Dignified and stately,

Dignified and stately,

Dignified and stately,
Dignified and stately!

CHORUS

Tho' our hearts she's badly bruising,
In another suitor choosing,
Let's pretend it's most amusing,
Let's pretend it's most amusing,

Ha, ha, ha! ha, ha, ha! ha, ha, ha!
Tan-ta-ra, tan-ta-ra, tan-ta-ra, tan-ta-ra!
Ra, ra, ra, ra!
Tan-ta-ra!
Tan-ta-ra!

(Exeunt all the Peers, marching round stage with much dignity.
LORD CHANCELLOR separates PHYLLIS from STREPHON
and orders her off. She follows Peers. Manent LORD CHANCEL-
LOR and STREPHON.)

LORD CH.

Now, sir, what excuse have you to offer for having disobeyed an order of
the Court of Chancery?

STREPHON

My Lord, I know no Courts of Chancery; I go by Nature's Acts of Parliament. The bees—the breeze—the seas—the rooks—the brooks—the
gales—the vales—the fountains and the mountains, cry, "You love this
maiden—take her, we command you!" 'Tis writ in heaven by the bright
barbed dart that leaps forth into lurid light from each grim thundercloud.
The very rain pours forth her sad and sodden sympathy! When chorussed
Nature bids me take my love, shall I reply, "Nay, but a certain Chancellor
forbids it?" Sir, you are England's Lord High Chancellor, but are you
Chancellor of birds and trees, King of the winds and Prince of thunder-
clouds?

LORD CH.

No. It's a nice point. I don't know that I ever met it before. But my difficulty
is that at present there's no evidence before the Court that chorussed
Nature has interested herself in the matter.

STREPHON

No evidence! You have my word for it. I tell you that she bade me take
my love.

LORD CH.

Ah! but my good sir, you mustn't tell us what she told you—it's not evidence. Now an affidavit from a thunderstorm, or a few words on oath from
a heavy shower, would meet with all the attention they deserve.

STREPHON

And have you the heart to apply the prosaic rules of evidence to a case
which bubbles over with poetical emotion?

LORD CH.

Distinctly. I have always kept my duty strictly before my eyes, and it is
to that fact that I owe my advancement to my present distinguished
position.

Music No. 12 SONG—(Lord Chancellor)

"When I went to the Bar."

When I went to the Bar as a very young man,
 (Said I to myself—said I,)
I'll work on a new and original plan,
 (Said I to myself—said I,)
I'll never assume that a rogue or a thief
Is a gentleman worthy implicit belief,
Because his attorney has sent me a brief,
 (Said I to myself—said I!)
Ere I go into court I will read my brief through,
 (Said I to myself—said I,)
And I'll never take work I'm unable to do,
 (Said I to myself—said I,)
My learned profession I'll never disgrace
By taking a fee with a grin on my face,
When I haven't been there to attend to the case,
 (Said I to myself—said I!)
I'll never throw dust in a juryman's eyes,
 (Said I to myself—said I,)
Or hoodwink a judge who is not over-wise,
 (Said I to myself—said I,)
Or assume that the witnesses summoned in force
In Exchequer, Queen's Bench, Common Pleas, or Divorce,
Have perjur'd themselves as a matter of course,
 (Said I to myself—said I!)
In other professions in which men engage,
 (Said I to myself—said I,)
The Army, the Navy, the Church, and the Stage
 (Said I to myself—said I,)
Professional licence, if carried too far,
Your chance of promotion will certainly mar—
And I fancy the rule might apply to the Bar,
 (Said I to myself—said I!)

Exit LORD CHANCELLOR
Enter IOLANTHE

STREPHON Oh, Phyllis, Phyllis! To be taken from you just as I was on the point of making you my own! Oh, it's too much—it is too much.

IOLANTHE (*to STREPHON, who is in tears*). My son in tears—and on his wedding day!

STREPHON My wedding day! Oh, mother, weep with me, for the Law has interposed between us, and the Lord Chancellor has separated us for ever.

IOLANTHE The Lord Chancellor! (*Aside.*) Oh, if he did but know!

STREPHON (*overhearing her*). If he did but know what?

IOLANTHE No matter! The Lord Chancellor has no power over you. Remember you are half a fairy. You can defy him—down to the waist.

STREPHON	Yes, but from the waist downwards he can commit me to prison for years! Of what avail is it that my body is free, if my legs are working out seven years' penal servitude?
IOLANTHE	True. But take heart—our Queen has promised you her special protection. I'll go to her and lay your peculiar case before her.
STREPHON	My beloved mother! how can I repay the debt I owe you?

Music No. 13 FINALE—ACT I—(Phyllis, Iolanthe, Queen, Leila, Celia, Strephon, Lord Toll., Lord Mount., Lord Chancellor, & Chorus of Fairies & Peers.)

(As it commences, the Peers appear at the back, advancing unseen and on tiptoe. LORD MOUNTARARAT and LORD TOLLOLLER lead PHYLLIS between them, who listens in horror to what she hears.)

STREPHON	(to IOLANTHE). When darkly looms the day. And all is dull and grey, To chase the gloom away, On thee I'll call!
PHYLLIS	(*speaking aside to LORD MOUNTARARAT*). What was that?
LORD MOUNT.	(*aside to PHYLLIS*). I think I heard him say, That on a rainy day, To while the time away, On her he'd call!
MALE CHORUS	We think we heard him say, That on a rainy day, To while the time away, On her he'd call!

(PHYLLIS, much agitated at her lover's supposed faithlessness.)

IOLANTHE	(*to STREPHON*). When tempests wreck thy bark, And all is drear and dark, If thou shouldst need an Ark, I'll give thee one!
PHYLLIS	(*speaking aside to LORD TOLLOLLER*). What was that?
LORD TOLL.	(*aside to PHYLLIS*). I heard the minx remark, She'd meet him after dark, Inside St. James's Park, And give him one!
MALE CHORUS	We heard the minx remark, She'd meet him after dark, Inside St. James's Park, And give him one!

PHYLLIS	IOLANTHE	LORD TOLL.	STREPHON
The prospect's very bad,	The prospect's not so bad,	The prospect's not so bad,	The prospect's not so bad,
My heart so sore and sad	Thy heart so sore and sad	My heart so sore and sad	My heart so sore and sad
Will never more be glad	May very soon be glad	May very soon be glad	May very soon be glad
As summer's sun!	As summer's sun!	As summer's sun!	As summer's sun!

PHYLLIS (Contd.)	IOLANTHE (Contd.)	LORD TOLL. (Contd.)	STREPHON (Contd.)
For when the sky is dark,	For when the sky is dark,	For when the sky is dark,	For when the sky is dark,
And tempests wreck his bark,	And tempests wreck thy bark,	And tempests wreck his bark,	And tempests wreck my bark,
If he should need an Ark,	If thou shouldst need an Ark,	If he should need an Ark,	If I should need an Ark,
She'll give him one,	I'll give thee one,	She'll give him one,	She'll give me one,

PHYLLIS	IOLANTHE	LORD TOLL.	LORD MOUNT.	STREPHON
Give him one, Ah, one!	Ah, give thee one, Ah, give thee one!	Ah, give him one, Ah, give him one!	Ah, give him one; give him one!	Ah, one!

PHYLLIS (*revealing herself*). Ah!

(IOLANTHE and STREPHON much confused.)

PHYLLIS Oh, shameless one, tremble!
Nay, do not endeavour
Thy fault to dissemble,
We part—and for ever!
I worshipp'd him blindly,
He worships another—

STREPHON Attend to me kindly,
This lady's my mother!

LORD TOLL. This lady's his *what?*

STREPHON This lady's my mother!

TENORS This lady's his *what?*

BASSES He says she's his mother!

TENORS & BASSES Ha, ha, ha, ha, ha, ha, ha, ha, ha!

(They point derisively to IOLANTHE, laughing heartily at her. She goes for protection to STREPHON.)

Enter LORD CHANCELLOR. IOLANTHE veils herself.

LORD CH. What means this mirth unseemly,
That shakes the listening earth?

LORD TOLL. The joke is good extremely,
And justifies our mirth.

LORD MOUNT. This gentleman is seen,
With a maid of seventeen,
A-taking of his *dolce far niente!*
And wonders he'd achieve,
For he asks us to believe
She's his mother—and he's nearly five-and-twenty!

18

| LORD CH. | (*sternly*). Recollect yourself, I pray,
And be careful what you say—
As the ancient Romans said, *festina lente*,
For I really do not see
How so young a girl could be
The mother of a man of five-and-twenty. |

CHORUS OF PEERS   Ha, ha, ha, ha, ha, ha, ha, ha, ha!

| STREPHON | My Lord, of evidence I have no dearth—
She is—has been—my mother from my birth! |

BALLAD.

In babyhood
Upon her lap I lay,
With infant food
She moisten-ed my clay;
Had she withheld
The succour she supplied,
By hunger quell'd,
Your Strephon might have died!

| LORD CH. | (*much moved*). Had that refreshment been denied,
Indeed our Strephon might have died! |

| CHORUS
OF PEERS | (*much affected*). Had that refreshment been denied,
Indeed our Strephon might have died! |

| LORD MOUNT. | But as she's not
His mother, it appears,
Why weep these hot
Unnecessary tears?
And by what laws
Should we, so joyously
Rejoice, because
Our Strephon did not die?
Oh, rather let us pipe our eye
Because our Strephon did not die! |

| CHORUS
OF PEERS | That's very true—let's pipe our eye
Because our Stephon did not die! |

(All weep. IOLANTHE, who has succeeded in hiding her face from the LORD CHANCELLOR, escapes unnoticed.)

| PHYLLIS | Go, trait'rous one—for ever we must part:
To one of you, my Lords, I give my heart! |

CHORUS OF PEERS   Oh, rapture!

| STREPHON | Hear me, Phyllis! |

CHORUS OF PEERS   Oh, rapture!

STREPHON	Ere you leave me!
PHYLLIS	Not a word—you did deceive me!
STREPHON	Hear me, Phyllis!
PHYLLIS	You did deceive me!
CHORUS OF PEERS	Not a word—you did deceive, you did deceive her!

Exit STREPHON

BALLAD—PHYLLIS

For riches and rank I do not long—
Their pleasures are false and vain;
I gave up the love of a lordly throng
For the love of a simple swain.
But now that simple swain's untrue,
With sorrowful heart I turn to you—
A heart that's aching, Quaking, breaking,
As sorrowful hearts are wont to do!
The riches and rank that you befall
Are the only baits you use,
So the richest and rankiest of you all
My sorrowful heart shall choose.
As none are so noble—none so rich
As this couple of lords, I'll find a niche
In my heart that's aching, Quaking, breaking,
For one of you two—and I don't care which!

ENSEMBLE

PHYLLIS	(*to LORD MOUNTARARAT and LORD TOLLOLLER*). To you I give my heart so rich!
ALL	(*puzzled*). To which?
PHYLLIS	I do not care! To you I yield—it is my doom!
ALL	To whom?
PHYLLIS	I'm not aware! I'm yours for life if you but choose.
ALL	She's whose?
PHYLLIS	That's your affair; I'll be a countess, shall I not?
ALL	Of what?
PHYLLIS	I do not care!

ALL	Lucky little lady!
	Strephon's lot is shady;
	Rank, it seems, is vital,
	"Countess" is the title,
	Yes, countess, countess the title, the title,
	But of what I'm not aware!
	But of what I'm not aware!

Enter STREPHON

STREPHON	Can I inactive see my fortunes fade?
	No, no!
PEERS	Ho, ho!
STREPHON	No, no!
PEERS	Ho! Ho!
STREPHON	Mighty protectress, hasten to my aid!

(Enter Fairies, tripping, headed by CELIA, LEILA, and FLETA and followed by QUEEN.)

CHORUS OF FAIRIES	Tripping hither, tripping thither,
	Nobody knows why or whither;
	Why you want us we don't know,
	But you've summon'd us, and so
	Enter all the little fairies
	To their usual tripping measure!
	To oblige you all our care is—
	Tell us, pray, what is your pleasure!
STREPHON	The lady of my love has caught me talking to another—
PEERS	Oh, fie! young Strephon is a rogue!
STREPHON	I tell her very plainly that the lady is my mother—
PEERS	Taradiddle, taradiddle, tol lol lay!
STREPHON	She won't believe my statement, and declares we must be parted,
	Because on a career of double-dealing I have started,
	Then gives her hand to one of these, and leaves me broken-hearted—
PEERS	Taradiddle, taradiddle, tol lol lay!
QUEEN	Ah, cruel ones, to separate two lovers from each other!
FAIRIES	Oh, fie! our Strephon's not a rogue!
QUEEN	You've done him an injustice, for the lady *is* his mother!

21

FAIRIES	Taradiddle, taradiddle, tol lol lay!
LORD CH.	That fable p'rhaps may serve his turn as well as any other.
	(*aside*) I didn't see her face, but if they fondled one another,
	And she's but seventeen—I don't believe it was his mother!
	(*aloud*) Taradiddle, taradiddle.
FAIRIES	Tol lol lay!
LORD TOLL.	I have often had a use
	For a thorough-bred excuse
	Of a sudden (which is English for "*repente*"),
	But of all I ever heard This is much the most absurd,
	For she's seventeen and he is five-and-twenty!

FAIRIES	**PEERS**
Tho' she is seventeen, and he is only five-and-twenty!	For she is seventeen, and he is only five-and-twenty!
Oh fie, our Strephon's not a rogue!	Oh fie, young Strephon is a rogue!

LORD MOUNT.	Now listen, pray, to me, For this paradox will be
	Carried nobody at all CONTRADICENTE.
	Her age, upon the date Of his birth was MINUS eight,
	If she's seventeen, and he is five-and-twenty!

FAIRIES & PEERS If she is seventeen and he is only five-and-twenty!

FAIRIES & ALL principals except QUEEN, IOLANTHE, & STREPHON	**PEERS**
To say she is his mother is an utter bit of folly!	To say she is his mother is an utter bit of folly!
Oh fie, our Strephon's not a rogue!	Oh fie, young Strephon is a rogue!

FAIRIES & PEERS, ETC.	Perhaps his brain is addled And it's very melancholy!
	Ta-ra-did-dle, ta-ra-did-dle, tol lol lay!
	I wouldn't say a word that could be reckoned as injurious,
	But to find a mother younger than her son is very curious,
	And that's a kind of mother that is usually spurious.
	Taradiddle, taradiddle, tol lol lay!
LORD CH.	Go away, madam; I should say, madam,
	You display, madam, Shocking taste.
	It is rude, madam, To intrude, madam,
	With your brood, madam, Brazen-faced!
	You come here, madam, Interfere, madam,
	With a peer, madam. (I am one.)
	You're aware, madam, What you dare, madam,
	So take care, madam, And begone!

CHORUS OF FAIRIES (To QUEEN).

Let us stay, madam, I should say, madam,
They display, madam, Shocking taste.
It is rude, madam, To allude, madam,
To your brood, madam, Brazen-faced!
We don't fear, madam, Any peer, madam,

CHORUS OF FAIRIES (To QUEEN) (contd.)
> Tho' my dear madam, This is one.
> They will stare, madam, When aware, madam,
> What they dare, madam—What they've done!

QUEEN
> (*aside, furiously*)
> Bearded by these puny mortals!
> I will launch from fairy portals
> All the most terrific thunders
> In my armoury of wonders!

PHYLLIS
> (*aside*)
> Should they launch terrific wonders,
> All would then repent their blunders!

PHYLLIS	QUEEN	FAIRIES	PEERS
		Let us	Go a-
Sure—ly	Bearded	stay, madam, I should	way, madam, I should
these must	by these	say, madam, They dis-	say, madam, You dis-
be im-	puny	play, madam, Shocking	play, madam, Shocking
mortals!	mortals!	taste. It is	taste. It is
Should they	I will	rude, madam, To al-	rude, madam, To in-
launch from	launch from	lude, madam, To your	trude, madam, With your
fairy	fairy	brood, madam, Brazen-	brood, madam, Brazen-
portals	portals	faced! We don't	faced! You come
All their	All the	fear, madam, Any	here, madam, Inter-
most ter-	most ter-	peer, madam, Tho', my	fere, madam, With a
rific	rific	dear madam, This is	peer, madam (I am
wonders,	thunders	one. They will	one). You're a-
We should	In my	stare, madam, When a-	ware, madam, What you
then re-	armour-	ware, madam, What they	dare, madam, So take
pent	y	dare, madam, When a-	care, madam, What you
our	of	ware, madam, What they've	dare, madam, And be-
blun - -	won - -	done! They will	gone! You're a-
- - - -	- - - -	stare, When a-	ware, What you
ders!	ders!	ware, What they	dare, So take
Should re—		dare, What they've	care, And be-

PHYLLIS & THREE SOPS	QUEEN	FAIRIES	PEERS
pent, - - -		done, madam, They will	gone! - - -
- - - - - -		stare, madam, When a-	- - - - - -
- - - - - -	My - - -	ware, madam, What they	- - - - - -
re—	- - - - - -	dare, madam, What they've	- - - - - -
pent - - -	ar—	done, madam, They will	- - - You're a-
- - - - - -	mour—	stare, madam, When a-	ware, madam, What you
- - - our	y of	ware, madam, What they	dare, madam, So take
blun-	won—	dare, madam, What they've	care, madam, And be—
ders!	ders!	done! They will	gone! You're a-
		stare, madam, When a-	ware, madam, What you
		ware, What they	dare, madam, So take
		dare, madam, What they've	care, madam, And be—
		done, madam, They will	gone, madam, You're a-
We should	They will	stare, madam, When a-	ware, madam, What you
then, should	soon, will	ware, madam, What they	dare, madam, So take

PHYLLIS & THREE SOPS (Contd.)	QUEEN (Contd.)	FAIRIES (Contd.)	PEERS (Contd.)
then re-pent!	soon re-pent!	dare, madam, What they've done!	care, madam, And be—gone!

Exit PHYLLIS

QUEEN　　Oh! Chancellor unwary, It's highly necessary
Your tongue to teach Respectful speech—
Your attitude to vary! Your badinage so airy,
Your manner arbitrary, Are out of place
When face to face With an influential Fairy.

ALL THE PEERS (*aside*) We never knew
We were talking to
An influential Fairy!

LORD CH.　　A plague on this vagary I'm in a nice quandary
Of hasty tone With dames unknown;
I ought to be more chary. It seems that she's a fairy
From Andersen's li-*bra*-ry.
And I took her for The proprietor
Of a Ladies' Seminary!

PEERS　　We took her for The proprietor
Of a Ladies' Seminary!

QUEEN　　When next your Houses do assemble,
You may tremble!

CELIA　　Our wrath, when gentlemen offend us,
Is tremendous!

LEILA　　They meet, who underrate our calling,
Doom appalling!

QUEEN　　Take down our sentence as we speak it,
And *he* shall wreak it! (Indicating STREPHON.)

PEERS　　Oh, spare us!

QUEEN　　Henceforth, Strephon, cast away
Crooks and pipes and ribbons so gay—
Flocks and herds that bleat and low!
Into Parliament you shall go!

FAIRIES &　　Into Parliament he shall go!
PEERS

Backed by $\genfrac{}{}{0pt}{}{\text{our}}{\text{their}}$ supreme authority,
He'll command a large majority;
Into Parliament, into Parliament,
Parliament, Parliament, he shall go!
Into Parliament he shall go!
Into Parliament, into Parliament,
Parliament, Parliament, he shall go!
Into Parliament he shall go!

QUEEN	In the Parliament'ry hive Lib'ral or Conservative Whig or Tory I don't know But into Parliament you shall go!
FAIRIES & **PEERS**	Into Parliament he shall go! Backed by _{their}^{our} supreme authority, He'll command a large majority:

FAIRIES	**PEERS**
Into Parliament,	Into Parliament
	P A rliament,
P A R Parliament,	

FAIRIES & **PEERS**	he shall go! Into Parliament he shall go! Into Parliament, into Parliament, Parliament, Parliament, he shall go! Into Parliament he shall go!

QUEEN		**PEERS**
(*speaking through music*) Every bill and every measure That may gratify his pleasure, Though your fury it arouses, Shall be passed by both your Houses!		
		Oh!
You shall sit, if he sees reason, Through the grouse and salmon season:		
		No!
He shall end the cherished rights You enjoy on Friday nights:		
		No! No!
He shall prick that annual blister, Marriage with deceased wife's sister:		
		Mercy!
Titles shall ennoble, then, All the Common Councilmen:		
		Spare us!
Peers shall teem in Christendom, And a Duke's exalted station Be attainable by Com- Petitive Examination!		

(Exeunt LORD CHANCELLOR, LORD MOUNTARARAT
& LORD TOLLOLLER)

PEERS	Oh, horror!
FAIRIES	Their horror! They can't dissemble! Now hide the fear that makes them tremble!

FAIRIES, QUEEN & STREPHON	**PEERS**
With Strephon for your foe, no doubt, A fearful prospect opens out, And who shall say What evils may Result in consequence.	Young Strephon is the kind of lout We do not care a fig about! We cannot say What evils may Result in consequence.

FAIRIES, QUEEN & STREPHON (Contd.)
A hideous vengeance will pursue
All noblemen who venture to
Oppose his views,
Or boldly choose
To offer him offence.
'Twill plunge them into grief and shame;
His kind forbearance they must claim,
If they'd escape
In any shape
A very painful wrench.

PEERS (Contd.)
But lordly vengeance will pursue
All kinds of common people who
Oppose our views,
Or boldly choose
To offer us offence.

PEERS   Your pow'rs we dauntlessly pooh-pooh:
A dire revenge will fall on you
If you besiege
Our high PRESTIGE.

FAIRIES, etc.   (The word "PRESTIGE" is French, The word "PRESTIGE" is French:)

FAIRIES, etc.
Although our threats you now pooh-pooh,
A dire revenge will fall on you.
With Strephon for your foe, no doubt,
A fearful prospect opens out!
And who shall say What evils may
Result in consequence?

PEERS
Your pow'rs we dauntlessly pooh-pooh,
A dire revenge will fall on you.
Young Strephon is the kind of lout
We do not care a fig about!
We cannot say What evils may
Result in consequence.

PEERS   Our lordly style
You shall not quench
With base *canaille!*

FAIRIES   (That word is French.)

PEERS   Distinction ebbs
Before a herd
Of vulgar *plebs!*

FAIRIES   (A Latin word.)

PEERS   'Twould fill with joy,
And madness stark
The ὁι πολλοι!

FAIRIES   (A Greek remark.)

PEERS   One Latin work, one Greek remark,
And one that's French.

FAIRIES   Your lordly style
We'll quickly quench
With base *canaille!*

PEERS   (That word is French.)

FAIRIES   Distinction ebbs
Before a herd
Of vulgar *plebs!*

PEERS	(A Latin word.)
FAIRIES	'Twill fill with joy And madness stark The ὁι πολλοι!
PEERS	(A Greek remark.)
FAIRIES	One Latin word, one Greek remark, And one that's French.

FAIRIES	**PEERS**
With Strephon for your foe, no doubt,	Young Strephon is the kind of lout
A fearful prospect opens out!	We do not care a fig about!
And who shall say What evils may	We cannot say What evils may
Result in consequence?	Result in consequence,
A hideous vengeance will pursue	But lordly vengeance will pursue
All noblemen who venture to	All kinds of common people who
Oppose his views, Or boldly choose	Oppose our views, Or boldly choose
To offer him offence. We will not	To offer us offence. You
wait,	needn't wait, A-
We go sky-	way you fly! Your
high!	threaten'd hate We
Our threaten'd	thus defy! You
hate	needn't wait, A-
You	way you fly! Your
won't	threaten'd hate We
de-	thus, we thus de-
fy! We will not wait, We go sky-high!	fy! You needn't wait, Away you fly!
Our threaten'd hate You won't defy!	Your threaten'd hate We thus defy!
Away we go! We go sky-high!	Away you go! You go sky-high!
Our threaten'd hate You won't defy!	Your threaten'd hate We thus defy!
You won't defy!	We thus defy!
You won't, you won't defy!	We thus, we thus defy!
You won't, you won't defy!	We thus, we thus defy!

(FAIRIES threaten PEERS with their wands. Enter PHYLLIS, followed by LORD CHANCELLOR, LORD MOUNT-ARARAT & LORD TOLLOLLER. She implores STRE-PHON to relent; he casts her from him, and she falls fainting into the arms of LORD MOUNTARARAT & LORD TOL-LOLLER.)

E N D   O F   A C T   1

ACT II

Music No. 1 SONG (Sentry)

"When all night long a chap remains"

SCENE.—*Palace Yard, Westminster. Westminster Hall, L. Clocktower up, R. C. PRIVATE WILLIS* discovered on sentry, R. Moonlight.

Song—Private Willis

When all night long a chap remains
On sentry-go, to chase monotony
He exercises of his brains,
That is, assuming that he's got any.
Though never nurtur'd in the lap
Of luxury, yet I admonish you,
I am an intellectual chap,
And think of things that would astonish you.
I often think it's comical—Fal, lal, la! Fal, lal, la!
How Nature always does contrive—Fal, lal, la, la!
That ev'ry boy and ev'ry gal
That's born into the world alive
Is either a little Liberal
Or else a little Conservative!

Fal, lal, la! Fal, la, la!
Is either a little Liberal,
Or else a little Conservative!
Fal, lal, la!

When in that House M.P.s divide,
If they've a brain and cerebellum, too,
They've got to leave that brain outside,
And vote just as their leaders tell 'em to.
But then the prospect of a lot
Of dull M.P.s in close proximity,
All thinking for themselves, is what
No man can face with equanimity.

Then let's rejoice with loud Fal lal
Fal, lal, la! Fal, lal, la!
That Nature always does contrive—Fal, lal, la, la!
That ev'ry boy and ev'ry gal
That's born into the world alive,
Is either a little Liberal,
Or else a little Conservative!
Fal, lal, la! Fal, lal, la!
Is either a little Liberal,
Or else a little Conservative!
Fal, lal, la!

Music No. 2 CHORUS OF FAIRIES AND PEERS

"Strephon's a Member of Parliament."

Enter Fairies, with CELIA, LEILA and FLETA. They trip round stage.

CHORUS OF FAIRIES

Strephon's a Member of Parliament!
Carries ev'ry Bill he chooses.
To his measures all assent—
Showing that fairies have their uses,
Whigs and Tories
Dim their glories,
Giving an ear to all his stories—
Lords and Commons are both in the blues:
Strephon makes them shake in their shoes!

1st SOPS
Shake in their shoes!

Shake in their shoes!

2nd SOPS

Shake in their shoes!

Shake in their shoes!

ALL FAIRIES   Strephon makes them shake in their shoes, in their shoes!

Enter Peers from Westminster Hall

CHORUS OF PEERS

Strephon's a Member of Parliament!
Running a-muck of all abuses.
His unqualified assent
Somehow nobody now refuses.
Whigs and Tories
Dim their glories,
Giving an ear to all his stories—
Carrying every Bill he may wish:
Here's a pretty kettle of fish!

TENORS
Kettle of fish

Kettle of fish

BASSES

Kettle of fish

Kettle of fish

ALL PEERS   Here's a pretty kettle, a kettle of fish!

FAIRIES &   Strephon's a Member of Parliament!
PEERS   Carries ev'ry Bill he chooses
To his measures all assent,
Carrying ev'ry Bill he may wish,
Carrying ev'ry Bill he may wish:
Here's a pretty kettle of fish!

Enter LORD MOUNTARARAT and LORD TOLLOLLER
from Westminster Hall.

CELIA   You seem annoyed.

LORD MOUNT.   Annoyed! I should think so! Why, this ridiculous *protégé* of yours is playing the deuce with everything! To-night is the second reading of his Bill to throw the Peerage open to Competitive Examination!

LORD TOLL.   And he'll carry it, too!

LORD MOUNT.   Carry it? Of course he will! He's a Parliamentary Pickford—he carries everything!

LEILA   Yes. If you please, that's our fault.

LORD MOUNT.   The deuce it is!

CELIA   Yes; we influence the members, and compel them to vote just as he wishes them to.

LEILA   It's our system. It shortens the debates.

LORD TOLL.   Well, but think what it all means. I don't so much mind for myself, but with a House of Peers with no grandfathers worth mentioning, the country must go to the dogs!

LEILA   I suppose it must!

LORD MOUNT.   I don't want to say a word against brains—I've a great respect for brains—I often wish I had some myself—but with a House of Peers composed exclusively of people of intellect, what's to become of the House of Commons?

LEILA   I never thought of that!

LORD MOUNT.   This comes of women interfering in politics. It so happens that if there is an institution in Great Britain which is not susceptible of any improvement at all: it is the House of Peers!

Music No. 3 SONG—(Lord Mountararat, with Chorus)

"When Britain really ruled the waves."

LORD MOUNT.   When Britain really rul'd the waves—
(In good Queen Bess's time)
The House of Peers made no pretence,
To intellectual eminence,
Or scholarship sublime;
Yet Britain won her proudest bays
In good Queen Bess's glorious days!
Yet Britain won her proudest bays
In good Queen Bess's glorious days.

CHORUS OF FAIRIES & PEERS
Yes, Britain won her proudest bays
In good Queen Bess's glorious days.

30

LORD MOUNT.   When Wellington thrash'd Bonaparte,
                As ev'ry child can tell,
                The House of Peers throughout the war,
                Did nothing in particular,
                And did it very well:
                Yet Britain set the world ablaze
                In good King George's glorious days!
                Yet Britain set the world ablaze
                In good King George's glorious days.

CHORUS   Yes, Britain set the world ablaze
                In good King George's glorious days.

LORD MOUNT.   And while the House of Peers with-holds
                Its legislative hand,
                And noble statesmen do not itch
                To interfere with matters which
                They do not understand,
                As bright will shine Great Britain's rays,
                As in King George's glorious days!
                As bright will shine Great Britain's rays,
                As in King George's glorious days.

CHORUS   As bright will shine Great Britain's rays,

LORD MOUNT.	**CHORUS**
In good King George's glorious days.	As in King George's glorious days.

LEILA   (who has been much attracted by the Peers during this song).
                Charming persons, are they not?

CELIA   Distinctly. For self-contained dignity, combined with airy condescension,
                give me a British Representative Peer!

LORD TOLL.   Then pray stop this *protégé* of yours before it's too late. Think of the mischief
                you're doing!

LEILA   But we *can't* stop him now. (Aside to CELIA). Aren't they lovely! (*Aloud*).
                Oh, why did you go and defy us, you great geese!

      Music No. 4   DUET. (Leila, Celia, with Chorus of Fairies, Lord Mountararat,
                  Lord Tolloller, & Chorus of Peers).

                "In vain to us you plead."

LEILA   In vain to us you plead—
                Don't go!
                Your pray'rs we do not heed—
                Don't go!
                It's true we sigh,
                But don't suppose
                A tearful eye
                Forgiveness shows.
                Oh, no!

LEILA (contd.)	We're very cross indeed— Yes, very cross. Don't go!
FAIRIES	It's true we sigh, But don't suppose A tearful eye Forgiveness shows. Oh no! We're very cross indeed, Yes, very cross, Don't go!
CELIA	Your disrespectful sneers— Don't go! Call forth indignant tears— Don't go! You break our laws— You are our foe: We cry, because We hate you so! *You* know! You very wicked Peers! You wicked Peers! Don't go!
FAIRIES	You break our laws, You are our foe: We cry because We hate you so! *You* know! You very wicked Peers! You wicked Peers, Don't go!
LORDS MOUNT. & TOLL.	Our disrespectful sneers, Ha, Ha! Call forth indignant tears, Ha, Ha! If that's the case, my dears—
FAIRIES	Don't go!
PEERS	We'll go!

(Exeunt LORD MOUNTARARAT, LORD TOLLOLLER, and Peers. Fairies gaze wistfully after them.)

Enter FAIRY QUEEN

QUEEN	Oh, shame—shame upon you! Is this your fidelity to the laws you are bound to obey? Know ye not that it is death to marry a mortal?
LEILA	Yes, but it's not death to *wish* to marry a mortal!

FLETA	If it were, you'd have to execute us all!
QUEEN	Oh, this is weakness! Subdue it!
CEILA	We know it's weakness, but the weakness is so strong!
LEILA	We are not all as tough as you are!
QUEEN	Tough! Do you suppose that I am insensible to the effect of manly beauty? Look at that man! *(Referring to sentry)*. A perfect picture! *(To sentry)*. Who are you, sir?
WILLIS	*(coming to "attention")*. Private Willis, B Company, 1st Grenadier Guards.
QUEEN	You're a very fine fellow, sir.
WILLIS	I am generally admired.
QUEEN	I can quite understand it. *(To Fairies)*. Now here is a man whose physical attributes are simply godlike. That man has a most extraordinary effect upon me. If I yielded to a natural impulse, I should fall down and worship that man. But I mortify this inclination. I wrestle with it, and it lies beneath my feet! That is how I treat my regard for that man!

Music No. 5 SONG. (Queen, with Chorus of Fairies)

"Oh, foolish fay."

FAIRY QUEEN	Oh, foolish fay, Think you, because His brave array My bosom thaws, I'd disobey Our fairy laws? Because I fly In realms above, In tendency To fall in love, Resemble I The am'rous dove? Resemble I The am'rous dove? Oh, am'rous dove! Type of Ovidius Naso! This heart of mine Is soft as thine, Although I dare not say so!
CHORUS	Oh, amorous dove! Type of Ovidius Naso!
QUEEN	This heart of mine Is soft as thine, Although I dare not say so! On fire that glows With heat intense I turn the hose Of common sense, And out it goes At small expense! We must maintain Our fairy law, That is the main On which to draw— In that we gain A Captain Shaw! In that we gain A Captain Shaw Oh, Captain Shaw! Type of true love kept under! Could thy Brigade With cold cascade Quench my great love I wonder!
CHORUS	Oh, Captain Shaw! Type of true love kept under!
QUEEN	Could thy Brigade With cold cascade

QUEEN	CHORUS
Quench my great love I	
won—	I Won—
der!	der!

(*Exeunt Fairies and* FAIRY QUEEN, *sorrowfully.*)

Enter PHYLLIS

PHYLLIS   (*half crying*). I can't think why I'm not in better spirits. I'm engaged to two noblemen at once. That ought to be enough to make any girl happy. But I'm miserable! Don't suppose it's because I care for Strephon, for I hate him! No girl *could* care for a man who goes about with a mother considerably younger than himself!

Enter LORD MOUNTARARAT and LORD TOLLOLLER

LORD MOUNT.   Phyllis! My darling

LORD TOLL.   Phyllis! My own!

PHYLLIS   Don't! How dare you? Oh, but perhaps you're the two noblemen I'm engaged to?

LORD MOUNT.   I am one of them.

LORD TOLL.   I am the other.

PHYLLIS   Oh, then, my darling (to LORD MOUNTARARAT). My own! (To LORD TOLLOLLER). Well, have you settled which it's to be?

LORD TOLL.   Not altogether. It's a difficult position. It would be hardly delicate to toss up. On the whole, we would rather leave it to you.

PHYLLIS   How can it possibly concern me? You are both Earls, and you are both rich, and you are both plain.

LORD MOUNT.   So we are. At least I am.

LORD TOLL.   So am I.

LORD MOUNT.   No, no!

LORD TOLL.   I am indeed. Very plain.

LORD MOUNT.   Well, well—perhaps you are.

PHYLLIS   There's really nothing to choose between you. If one of you would forego his title, and distribute his estates among his Irish tenantry, why then I should then see a reason for accepting the other.

LORD MOUNT.   Tolloller, are you prepared to make this sacrifice?

LORD TOLL.   No!

LORD MOUNT.	Not even to oblige a lady?
LORD TOLL.	No! not even to oblige a lady.
LORD MOUNT.	Then, the only question is, which of us shall give way to the other? Perhaps, on the whole, she would be happier with me. I don't know. I may be wrong.
LORD TOLL.	No. I don't know that you are. I really believe she would. But the awkward part of the thing is that if you rob me of the girl of my heart, we must fight, and one of us must die. It's a family tradition that I have sworn to respect. It's a painful position, for I have a very strong regard for you, George.
LORD MOUNT.	(*much affected*). My dear Thomas!
LORD TOLL.	You are very dear to me, George. We were boys together—at least *I* was. If I were to survive you, my existence would be hopelessly embittered.
LORD MOUNT.	Then, my dear Thomas, you must not do it. I say it again and again—if it will have this effect upon you, you must not do it. No, no. If one of us is to destroy the other, let it be me!
LORD TOLL.	No, no!
LORD MOUNT.	Ah, yes!—by our boyish friendship I implore you!
LORD TOLL.	(*much moved*). Well, well, be it so, But, no—no! I cannot consent to an act which would crush you with unavailing remorse.
LORD MOUNT.	But it would not do so. I should be very sad at first—oh, who would not be?—but it would wear off. I like you *very much*—but not, perhaps, as much as you like me.
LORD TOLL.	George, you're a noble fellow, but that tell-tale tear betrays you. No, George; you are very fond of me, and I cannot consent to give you a week's uneasiness on my account.
LORD MOUNT.	But, dear Thomas, it would not last a week! Remember, you lead the House of Lords; on your demise I shall take your place! Oh, Thomas, it would not last a day!
PHYLLIS	(*coming down*). Now, I do hope you're not going to fight about me, because it's really not worth while.
LORD TOLL.	(*looking at her*). Well, I don't believe it is!
LORD MOUNT.	Nor I. The sacred ties of friendship are paramount.
Music No. 6	QUARTET. (Phyllis, Lord Tolloller, Lord Mountararat, & Sentry.)
	"Tho' p'r'aps I may incur your blame."
LORD TOLL.	Though p'r'aps I may incur your blame, The things are few I would not do In Friendship's name!

35

LORD MOUNT.	And I may say I think the same; Not even love Should rank above True Friendship's name!
PHYLLIS	Then free me, pray; be mine the blame; Forget your craze And go your ways In Friendship's name—In Friendship's name!
ALL	Oh, many a man, in Friendship's name, Has yielded fortune, rank and fame! But no one yet, in the world so wide, Has yielded up a promised bride!
WILLIS	Accept, oh Friendship, all the same,
ALL	This sacrifice to thy dear name! Accept this sacrifice to thy dear name!

(Exeunt LORD MOUNTARARAT and LORD TOLLOLLER, loving-
ly, in one direction, and PHYLLIS in another. Exit Sentry.)

Enter LORD CHANCELLOR, very miserable.

Music No. 7 RECITATIVE & SONG. (Lord Chancellor)

"Love unrequited robs me of my rest."
Love, unrequited, robs me of my rest;
Love, hopeless love, my ardent soul encumbers;
Love, nightmare-like, lies heavy on my chest,
And weaves itself into my midnight slumbers!

Song—Lord Chancellor

When you're lying awake with a dismal headache, and repose is taboo'd
        by anxiety,
I conceive you may use any language you choose to indulge in, without
        impropriety;
For your brain is on fire—the bedclothes conspire of usual slumber to
        plunder you:
First your counterpane goes, and uncovers your toes, and your sheet slips
        demurely from under you;
Then the blanketing tickles—you feel like mixed pickles—so terribly
        sharp is the pricking,
And you're hot, and you're cross, and you tumble and toss till there's
        nothing 'twixt you and the ticking,
Then the bedclothes all creep to the ground in a heap, and you pick 'em
        all up in a tangle;
Next your pillow resigns and politely declines to remain at its usual
        angle!
Well, you get some repose in the form of a doze, with hot eye-balls and
        head ever aching,
But your slumbering teems with such horrible dreams that you'd very
        much better be waking.
For you dream you are crossing the Channel, and tossing about in a
        steamer from Harwich—

36

LORD CH.
(Contd.)
	Which is something between a large bathing machine and a very small
	    second-class carriage—
	And you're giving a treat (penny ice and cold meat) to a party of friends
	    and relations—
	They're a ravenous horde—and they all came on board at Sloane Square
	    and South Kensington Stations.
	And bound on that journey you find your attorney (who started that
	    morning from Devon);
	He's a bit undersiz'd, and you don't feel surpris'd when he tells you he's
	    only eleven.
	Well, you're driving like mad with this singular lad (bye-the-bye the
	    ship's now a four-wheeler),
	And you're playing round games, and he calls you bad names when you
	    tell him that "ties pay the dealer";
	But this you can't stand, so you throw up your hand, and you find you're
	    as cold as an icicle,
	In your shirt and your socks (the black silk with gold clocks,) crossing
	    Sal'sbury Plain on a bicycle:
	And he and the crew are on bicycles, too—which they've somehow or
	    other invested in—
	And he's telling the tars, all the particu*lars* of a company he's interested
	    in—
	It's a scheme of devices, to get at low prices, all goods from cough mixtures
	    to cables
	(Which tickled the sailors) by treating retailers, as though they were all
	    vege*t*ables—
	You get a good spadesman to plant a small tradesman (first take off his
	    boots with a boot-tree),
	And his legs will take root, and his fingers will shoot, and they'll blossom
	    and bud like a fruit-tree,
	From the greengrocer tree you get grapes and green pea, cauliflower,
	    pineapple and cranberries,
	While the pastrycook plant, cherry brandy will grant, apple puffs, and
	    three-corners, and Banburys—
	The shares are a penny, and ever so many are taken by Rothschild and
	    Baring,
	And just as a few are allotted to you, you awake with a shudder despair-
	    ing—
	You're a regular wreck, with a crick in your neck, and no wonder you
	snore, for your head's on the floor, and you've needles and pins from your
	soles to your shins, and your flesh is a-creep, for your left leg's asleep, and
	you've cramp in your toes, and a fly on your nose, and some fluff in your
	lung, and a feverish tongue, and a thirst that's intense, and a general
	sense that you haven't been sleeping in clover; But the darkness has passed,
	and it's daylight at last, and the night has been long—ditto, my song—and
	thank goodness they're both of them over!

(LORD CHANCELLOR falls exhausted on a seat.)

Enter LORDS MOUNTARARAT and TOLLOLLER

LORD MOUNT.	I am much distressed to see your Lordship in this condition.
LORD CH.	Ah, my Lords, it is seldom that a Lord Chancellor has reason to envy the position of another, but I am free to confess that I would rather be

LORD CH. (**contd.**)	two Earls engaged to Phyllis than any other half-dozen noblemen upon the face of the globe.
LORD TOLL.	(*without enthusiasm*). Yes, it's an enviable position when you're the only one.
LORD MOUNT.	Oh, yes, no doubt—most enviable. At the same time, seeing you thus, we naturally say to ourselves, "This is very sad. His Lordship is constitutionally as blithe as a bird—he trills upon the bench like a thing of song and gladness. His series of judgments in F sharp minor, given *andante* in six-eight time, are among the most remarkable effects ever produced in a Court of Chancery. He is, perhaps, the only living instance of a judge whose decrees have received the honour of a double *encore*. How can we bring ourselves to do that which will deprive the Court of Chancery of one of its most attractive features?"
LORD CH.	I feel the force of your remarks, but I am here in two capacities, and they clash, my Lords, they clash! I deeply grieve to say that in declining to entertain my last application to myself, I presumed to address myself in terms which render it impossible for me ever to apply to myself again. It was a most painful scene, my Lords—most painful!
LORD TOLL.	This is what it is to have two capacities! Let us be thankful that we are persons of no capacity whatever.
LORD MOUNT.	Come, come. Remember you are a very just and kindly old gentleman, and you need have no hesitation in approaching yourself, so that you do so respectfully and with a proper show of deference.
LORD CH.	Do you really think so?
LORD MOUNT.	I do.
LORD CH.	Well, I will nerve myself to another effort, and, if that fails, I resign myself to my fate!

Music No. 8 TRIO. (Lord Tolloller, Lord Mountararat, & Lord Chancellor)

"If you go in you're sure to win."

LORD MOUNT.	If you go in you're sure to win— Yours will be the charming maidie: Be your law the ancient saw, "Faint heart never won fair lady!"
ALL	Never, never, never. Faint heart never won fair lady! Ev'ry journey has an end— When at the worst affairs will mend— Dark the dawn when day is nigh— Hustle your horse and don't say die!
LORD TOLL.	He who shies at such a prize Is not worth a maravedi, Be so kind to bear in mind— Faint heart never won fair lady!

ALL	Never, never, never.
	Faint heart never won fair lady!
	While the sun shines make your hay—
	Where a will is, there's a way—
	Beard the lion in his lair–
	None but the brave deserve the fair!
LORD CH.	I'll take heart and make a start—
	Though I fear the prospect's shady—
	Much I'd spend to gain my end—
	Faint heart never won fair lady!
ALL	Never, never, never.
	Faint heart never won fair lady!
	Nothing venture, nothing win—
	Blood is thick, but water's thin—
	In for a penny, in for a pound—
	It's Love that makes the world go round!
	Nothing venture, nothing win—
	Blood is thick, but water's thin—
	In for a penny, in for a pound—
	It's Love that makes the world go round!

(Dance, and exeunt arm-in-arm together.)

Enter STREPHON, in very low spirits.

STREPHON	I suppose one ought to enjoy oneself in Parliament, when one leads both Parties, as I do! But I'm miserable, poor, broken-hearted fool that I am! Oh, Phyllis, Phyllis!—

Enter PHYLLIS

PHYLLIS	Yes.
STREPHON	(*surprised*): Phyllis! But I suppose I should say "My Lady." I have not yet been informed which title your ladyship has pleased to select?
PHYLLIS	I—I haven't quite decided. You see, *I* have no *mother* to advise *me*!
STREPHON	No. I have.
PHYLLIS	Yes, a *young* mother.
STREPHON	Not very—a couple of centuries or so.
PHYLLIS	Oh! She wears well.
STREPHON	She does. She's a fairy.
PHYLLIS	I beg your pardon—a what?
STREPHON	Oh, I've no longer any reason to conceal the fact—she's a fairy.

PHYLLIS	A fairy! Well, but—that would account for a good many things! Then—I suppose *you're* a fairy?
STREPHON	I'm half a fairy.
PHYLLIS	Which half?
STREPHON	The upper half—down to the waistcoat.
PHYLLIS	Dear me! (*Prodding him with her fingers.*) There is nothing to show it!
STREPHON	Don't do that.
PHYLLIS	But why didn't you tell me this before?
STREPHON	I thought you would take a dislike to me. But as it's all off, you may as well know the truth—I'm only half a mortal.
PHYLLIS	But I'd rather have half a mortal I do love than half a dozen I don't!
STREPHON	Oh, I think not—go to your half-dozen.
PHYLLIS	It's only two, and I hate 'em. Please forgive me!
STREPHON	I don't think I ought to. Besides, all sorts of difficulties will arise. You know, my grandmother looks quite as young as my mother. So do all my aunts.
PHYLLIS	I quite understand. Whenever I see you kissing a very young lady I shall know it's an elderly relative.
STREPHON	You will? Then, Phyllis, I think we shall be very happy! (*Embracing her*).
PHYLLIS	We won't wait long.
STREPHON	No. We might change our minds. We'll get married first.
PHYLLIS	And change our minds afterwards?
STREPHON	That's the usual course.

Music No. 9 DUET. (Phyllis & Strephon)

"If we're weak enough to tarry."

STREPHON	If we're weak enough to tarry ere we marry,
	You and I,
	Of the feeling I inspire, you may tire
	By-and-bye.
	For peers with flowing coffers press their offers—
	That is why
	I am sure we should not tarry ere we marry,
	You and I!

PHYLLIS	If we're weak enough to tarry ere we marry,
	You and I,
	With a more attractive maiden, jewel-laden,
	You may fly.
	If by chance we should be parted, broken-hearted
	I should die—
	So I think we will not tarry ere we marry,
	You and I.

PHYLLIS	STREPHON
Ah,	Ah,
Ah,	If we're weak enough to tarry
If we're weak enough to tarry	Ere we marry, You and I,
Ere we marry, You and I,	Of the feeling I inspire,
With a more attractive maiden,	You may tire By-and-bye,
Jewel-laden, You may fly.	Of the feeling I inspire,
You—and	You may tire By-and-bye,
I, -------	If we're weak enough to tarry
If we're weak enough to tarry	Ere we marry, You and I,
Ere we marry, You and I,	Of the feeling I inspire
With a more attractive maiden,	You may tire By-and-bye.
Jewel-laden, You may fly.	

BOTH	So I think we will not tarry
	Ere we marry, Ere we marry,
	You and I, You and I, You and I.
PHYLLIS	But does your mother know you're—I mean, is she aware of our engagement?

Enter IOLANTHE

IOLANTHE	She is; and thus she welcomes her daughter-in-law! (Kisses her).
PHYLLIS	She kisses just like other people! But the Lord Chancellor?
STREPHON	I forgot him! Mother, none can resist your fairy eloquence; you will go to him and plead for us?
IOLANTHE	(*much agitated*). No, no; impossible!
STREPHON	But our happiness—our very lives—depend upon our obtaining his consent!
PHYLLIS	Oh, madam, you cannot refuse to do this!
IOLANTHE	You know not what you ask! The Lord Chancellor is—my husband!
STREPHON and PHYLLIS	Your husband!
IOLANTHE	My husband and your father! (Addressing STREPHON, who is much moved).
PHYLLIS	Then our course is plain; on his learning that Strephon is his son, all objection to our marriage will be at once removed!

IOLANTHE	No; he must never know! He believes me to have died childless, and, dearly as I love him, I am bound, under penalty of death, not to un- deceive him. But see—he comes! Quick my veil!

(IOLANTHE veils herself. STREPHON and PHYLLIS go off on tip-toe.)

Enter LORD CHANCELLOR

LORD CH.	Victory! Victory! Success has crowned my efforts, and I may consider myself engaged to Phyllis! At first I wouldn't hear of it—it was out of the question. But I took heart. I pointed out to myself that I was no stranger to myself; that, in point of fact, I had been personally acquainted with myself for some years. This had its effect. I admitted that I had watched my professional advancement with considerable interest; and I hand- somely added that I yielded to no one in admiration for my private and professional virtues. This was a great point gained. I then endeavoured to work upon my feelings. Conceive my joy when I distinctly perceived a tear glistening in my own eye! Eventually, after a severe struggle with myself, I reluctantly—most reluctantly—consented.

(IOLANTHE comes down veiled.)

Music No. 10 RECITATIVE & BALLAD. (Iolanthe)

"My lord, a suppliant at your feet."

IOLANTHE	My lord, a suppliant at your feet I kneel, Oh, listen to a mother's fond appeal! Hear me to-night! I come in urgent need— 'Tis for my son, young Strephon, that I plead!

BALLAD—IOLANTHE

He loves! If in the bygone years
Thine eyes have ever shed
Tears—bitter, unavailing tears,
For one untimely dead—
If, in the eventide of life
Sad thoughts of her arise,
Then let the mem'ry of thy wife
Plead for my boy—he dies!
He dies! If fondly laid aside
In some old cabinet,
Memorials of thy long-dead bride
Lie, dearly treasur'd yet,
Then let their hallow'd bridal dress—
Her little dainty gloves—
Her wither'd flowers—her faded tress—
Plead for my boy—he loves!

(The LORD CHANCELLOR is moved by this appeal. After a pause:)

Music No. 11 RECITATIVE. (Iolanthe, Queen, Lord Chancellor & Fairies)

"It may not be."

LORD CH.	It may not be—for so the fates decide! Learn thou that Phyllis is my promised bride.
IOLANTHE	*(in horror)*. Thy bride! No! no!
LORD CH.	It shall be so! Those who would separate us woe betide.
IOLANTHE	My doom thy lips have spoken— I plead in vain!
CHORUS OF FAIRIES (without).	Forbear! forbear!
IOLANTHE	A vow already broken. I break again!
CHORUS OF FAIRIES (without).	Forbear! forbear!
IOLANTHE	For him—for her—for thee I yield my life. Behold—it may not be! I am thy wife. *(Kneels.)*
CHORUS OF FAIRIES (without).	Aia-iah! Aia-iah! Aia-iah! Aia-iah! Wil-la-loo! Wil-la-loo!
LORD CH.	*(recognising her)*. Iolanthe! thou livest?
IOLANTHE	Aye! I live! Now let me die!

Enter FAIRY QUEEN and Fairies

QUEEN	Once again thy vows are broken: Thou thyself thy doom hast spoken!
FAIRIES	Aia-iah! Aia-iah! Aia-iah! Aia-iah! Willahalah! Willaloo! Willahalah! Willaloo!
QUEEN	Bow thy head to Destiny: Death thy doom, and thou shalt die!
FAIRIES	Aia-iah! Aia-iah! Aia-iah! Aia-iah! Willahalah! Willaloo! Willahalah! Willaloo!

(Peers and Sentry enter, The Queen raises her spear)

43

LEILA	Hold! If Iolanthe must die, so must we all; for, as she has sinned, so have we!
QUEEN	What!
CELIA	We are all fairy duchesses, marchionesses, countesses, viscountesses, and baronesses.
LORD MOUNT.	It's our fault. They couldn't help themselves.
QUEEN	It seems they *have* helped themselves, and pretty freely, too! (*After a pause*). You have all incurred death; but I can't slaughter the whole company! And yet (*unfolding a scroll*) the law is clear—every fairy must die who marries a mortal!
LORD CH.	Allow me, as an old equity draughtsman, to make a suggestion. The subtleties of the legal mind are equal to the emergency. The thing is really quite simple—the insertion of a single word will do it. Let it stand that every fairy shall die who don't marry a mortal, and there you are, out of your difficulty at once!
QUEEN	We like your humour. Very well! (*Altering the MS. in pencil*). Private Willis!
SENTRY	(*coming forward*). Ma'am!
QUEEN	To save my life, it is necessary that I marry at once. How would you like to be a fairy guardsman?
SENTRY	Well, ma'am, I don't think much of the British soldier who wouldn't ill-convenience himself to save a female in distress.
QUEEN	You are a brave fellow. You're a fairy from this moment. (*Wings spring from Sentry's shoulders*). And you, my Lords, how say you? Will you join our ranks?

(PHYLLIS and STREPHON enter)

(Fairies kneel to Peers and implore them to do so.)

LORD MOUNT.	(to LORD TOLLOLLER). Well, now that the Peers are to be recruited entirely from persons of intelligence, I really don't see what use *we* are down here, do you, Tolloller?
LORD TOLL.	None whatever.
QUEEN	Good! (*Wings spring from the shoulders of Peers*). Then away we go to Fairyland.

Music No. 12 FINALE. (Phyllis, Iolanthe, Queen, Leila, Celia, Lord Tolloller, Lord Mountararat, Strephon, Lord Chancellor, & Chorus of Fairies & Peers)

"Soon as we may, off and away."

PHYLLIS
Soon as we may, Off and away!
We'll commence our journey airy—
Happy are we—As you can see,
Ev'ry one is now a fairy!

PHYLLIS, IOLANTHE, & QUEEN
Ev'ry, ev'ry, ev'ry
Ev'ry one is now a fairy!
Tho' as a gen'ral rule we know
Two strings go to ev'ry bow,
Make up your minds that grief 'twill bring,
If you've two beaux to ev'ry string.

ALL
Though as a gen'ral rule we know
Two strings go to ev'ry bow,
Make up your minds that grief 'twill bring,
If you've two beaux to ev'ry string.

LORD CH.
Up in the sky, Ever so high,
Pleasures come in endless series;
We will arrange Happy exchange—
House of Peers for House of Peris!

LORD CH., LORD TOLL., & LORD MOUNT.
Peris, Peris, Peris,
House of Peers for House of Peris!
Up in the air sky high, sky high,
Free from Wards in Chancery,

LORD CHANCELLOR
I shall be surely happier, for
I'm such a susceptible Chancellor!

LORDS TOLL. & MOUNT.
He will be surely happier, for
He's such a susceptible Chancellor!

ALL
Up in the air, sky high, sky high,
Free from Wards in Chancery,
He will be surely happier for
He's such a susceptible Chancellor!

CURTAIN

Printed and bound in Great Britain